CREATING

SHARED

VISION

CREATING SHARED VISION

MARJORIE PARKER

DIALOG INTERNATIONAL LTD.

Book Design: Nancy Churchill

Illustrations and Cover Design: Kurt Davis

Cover painting: Svein Aarseth

Paintings of KF Garden: Siggen Falkeid

The writing was partly funded by the Norwegian Council for Scientific and Industrial Research (NTNF), Oslo, Norway.

ISBN 0-9630000-0-4

New and Expanded. First US Edition 1 2 3 4 5 6 7 8 9 10

To Per and Dag Olav who encourage me daily to live the lesson of my father, Robert L. Parker. His lesson was: you must use your imagination to bring into being new possibilities.

CONTENTS

ACKNOWLEDGEMENTS

This book is about vision and it is with gratitude that I thank those people who have contributed their vision to the realization of this book.

First and foremost, I would like to thank Michelle Czuba who, with her intuition and confidence, first convinced me that my story was worth publishing and who in the process of sharing her vision with me has become a valued friend.

I would like to thank W. Christopher Musselwhite and Sheryl Erickson for believing in the potential of this story and encouraging me to publish it in the United States.

I am grateful for the enthusiasm, insightful criticism, and knowledge that Eileen Sullivan and Andrea Meyer have brought to this project.

I am indebted to Per Grøholt, my husband and business partner, for his professional and personal support. Without him, this book might never have been completed.

Finally, I would like to thank the people in my life, past and present, who have helped me realize the strength of my own visions. I owe a great debt of gratitude to all and offer my sincere thanks.

FOREWORD

The authoritarian model has dominated western management for hundreds of years. Most books about vision are based on the authoritarian model. The focus has been on one or two top leaders who formulated a corporate vision and then announced it to the organization.

Marjorie Parker's book is different. It takes us away from authoritarian models and provides insight to what makes a learning organization. A learning organization is an organization that is continually expanding its capacity to create its future. The shift from authoritarian to learning organizations must start with learning how to create shared vision.

Creating Shared Vision portrays the process of groups of people sharing responsibility for creating an organization's vision. It takes courage and heart for a leader to engage others in visioning. Ms. Parker's book elequently shows how we can move along this path toward heightening everyone's genuine sense of influence and ownership of their organization. *Creating Shared Vision* is a welcome addition to other books that address vision. It is the first of its kind. The author leaves theory behind as she shares fears and uncertainties that only an honest account of a practical example can elicit.

The story told in *Creating Shared Vision* is fascinating. It should be mandatory reading for those interested in revitalizing their organizations and in moving toward becoming learning organizations.

Peter M. Senge

Peter M. Senge, Director, Organizational Learning Center, Massachusetts Institute of Technology, Sloan School of Management, Cambridge, Massachusetts, author of *The Fifth Discipline*.

PREFACE

This book was written partly as a testament to the potential of shared vision and partly as a testament to the people who had the courage to revitalize their organization through shared vision.

This is not a case study, a research document, or a how-to book. This is not a personal or organizational success story. This is simply the story of an organization's pioneering experience involving employees in the creation of its vision.

My experiences with shared vision have convinced me that there are better ways. There are better ways for us to move forward as individuals, families, companies, countries, and as a world community.

This story but casts a light on the vast potential of shared vision. It is my hope, that in sharing this story, individuals, consultants, business leaders, government leaders, and others may recognize that shared vision is about taking responsibility for and shaping the future. It is my hope that this story might serve as an inspiration for practical and down-to-earth people to risk making the commitment to creating and sustaining shared vision.

INTRODUCING VISION

In recent years there has been extensive media coverage of the achievements of visionary leaders. Almost daily the press identifies the need for visionary leaders in government, education, healthcare ,and business.

Many managers recognize the need to be visionary, yet lack an understanding of vision. This has resulted in managers focusing on formulating vision statements, rather than experiencing vision. It is not enough to recognize a need to be visionary. Managers need to better understand the nature of visions and what enhances and sustains them.

Some believe that a vision is just a dream, a flight from reality, wishful thinking, naive idealism, or merely idle fantasy. Some believe that the only persons having worthy visions are religious prophets, inventors, clairvoyants, or charismatic political and business leaders.

I believe people experience vision differently. Some hear it in sounds, some feel it, many experience it as mental images, still others sense it intuitively. In my work with organizations,I have observed that most commonly, visions are experienced and talked about as mental images. Visions are powerful mental images of what we want to create in the future.

They reflect what we care about most, and are harmonious with our values and sense of purpose.

Visions are the product of the head and the heart working together. As such, vision is much more than a mental image, and visioning is more than a mental process.

Visions are rooted in reality but focused on the future. Visions enable us to explore possibilities. They are desired realities.   While vision directs us toward the future, it is experienced in the present.

The tension we feel from comparing a mental image of a desired future with today's reality is what fuels a vision. Powerful visions can never be an escape from reality. Without an ongoing awareness of today's reality, visions become powerless.

The visioning process creates a magnetic field with the pull being away from today and toward the vision. The magnetism of a vision is generated from an integration of an individual's and organization's sense of purpose, values, uniqueness, and interaction with the physical, social, business, and political environments.

Visions are our deepest expressions of what we want to create. They are compelling and provide an overarching framework which guides us in making choices — choices that will transform our visions into today's realities.

A shared vision brings people together. It unites and provides the link between diverse people and activities. Shared visions are expressions of what people have in common, of what they, in community are committed to. People with shared vision are more likely to take responsibility; they are more likely to challenge the bounds of convention.

Any group of people can create a shared vision. Any challenge can be the focus of shared vision. Shared vision can be used whenever there is a need for change. Without shared vision, new ways of thinking or acting are inhibited by the pull of the status quo.

I believe that every individual has the capacity to vision. I feel that popular myths about visioning and traditional thinking patterns have prevented people from activating their innate capacity to vision.

In recent years the literature describing the importance of vision in leadership, organizational transformation, strategy, peak performance, and innovation has increased significantly. Although this is true, few if any examples exist of organizations involving employees on an extensive scale in visioning. The exception is Hydro Aluminum Karmøy Fabrikker (KF), a truly pioneering effort.

This book is the story of my experiences using shared visioning as an approach to organizational revitalization. It is the story of the two years I worked as a consultant with KF.

THE SETTING

HYDRO ALUMINUM KARMØY FABRIKKER

N orsk Hydro is Norway's largest industrial group. The group has interests in agriculture, oil and gas, petrochemicals, biomedicine, aquaculture, and light metals. The aluminum activities of Norsk Hydro merged with Årdal-Sunndal Verk in 1987 to form Hydro Aluminum.

As Europe's largest producer of aluminum, Hydro Aluminum employs more than 12,000 at 50 production plants in 10 countries. KF is the largest of Hydro Aluminum's plants. In 1986 it employed 1700 people. Aluminum was first produced there in 1967. KF was an independent company until 1975 when it was purchased by Norsk Hydro.

KF was in a state of crisis, entering the 1980s. The plant was non-profitable. It was consuming large amounts of energy and polluting the environment with huge emission clouds. It was a costly and unclean plant. KF had imported state-of-the-art Japanese technology, but lacked the necessary skills to make it effective. Within KF, the relationship between management and unions was combative. They were working against rather than with one another. The outlook for KF was dim.

In 1981, KF set in motion a project called, "We want to be better." Technical competencies were improved through systematic training and skill development. Quality and service became the focus.

Management and union leaders worked to open lines of communication. Together they decided which indicators they would track to see what progress was being made. They decided to monitor: plant cleanliness, absenteeism, safety, productivity, and the amount of employee suggestions.

Great strides were made. The workers and managers were successful in turning the plant around. They learned to trust one another. By 1985, KF was a profitable plant. It was attracting attention as a company committed to employee development and to a cleaner environment.

KF's ORGANIZATIONAL STRUCTURE

The organizational structure that existed at KF in 1986 consisted of four business units: Reduction Plant, Extrusion Plant, Rolling Mill, and Hydal (semi-fabrication). Each unit was financially independent from the others.

Every business unit has Working Committees. The Technical Services Department and the support departments: Personnel, Accounting, Information, Data, and Research & Development, likewise have Working Committees. These committees are advisory in nature and are composed of an equal number of elected union representatives and managers.

Working Committees have representatives on the Karmøy Advisory Board. The Karmøy Advisory Board meets monthly and traditionally addressed common plant concerns.   In addition, the Advisory Board organizes a biennial conference (BU Conference) for the 130 members from all of KF's Working Committees.

Advisory Boards and Working Committees are among the by-products of industrial democracy. In Norway industrial democracy is more than an ideal, it's the law. A portion of the 1935 Basic Agreement between the Employer's Confederation and the Trade Unions reads:

"Through cooperation and codetermination, employees will contribute their experience and insights to the creation of the financial conditions necessary for the continued development of the enterprise and for secure and satisfying working conditions, for the benefit of both the enterprise and its employees".

Since the war, the scope of the Basic Agreement has expanded. Today, a company is obliged to inform the workers about all changes that affect employees. Changes that are initiated without first informing workers constitute a breach of contract. All interventions carried out at KF were within, and enhanced by the framework of industrial democracy.

THE STORY

THE STORY BEGINS

An initial consultant/client meeting is like a blind date; exciting, yet anxiety provoking. Either the chemistry is there or it isn't. When it's present, there is the excitement without the anxiety. When it's not, the anxiety lingers.

My initial meeting brought me to a hotel conference room a short drive from KF on a chilly October morning in 1986. I was to meet Tormod Bjørk, the new managing director of the Karmøy plant, and Inger Tafjord, the manager of the Training Department. Tafjord initiated the meeting as she was familiar with my work using creative thinking in developing organizational strategies. The purpose of the meeting was to become acquainted, for me to gain some impressions of the challenges facing Bjørk, and to consider possibilities for dealing with them.

It didn't take long for me to know that the chemistry was there. Without this, what followed may never have happened. It enabled Bjørk with increasing ease to verbalize those things he cared about most and it enabled me to confidently pursue them.

Both Tafjord and Bjørk believed that KF was ready to begin a process that would allow the employees to maximize their creative potential.

There was an expressed restlessness in the organization. Having successfully worked together to resolve difficult past problems, there was a relatively high level of trust between unions and management.

Tormod Bjørk had only recently been named managing director. Bjørk, a 16 year veteran of KF, was not perceived as a leader seeking personal gain. He was viewed as a leader who would use power with the best interest of the organization in mind. Although not perceived as either charismatic or visionary, the consensus was that Bjørk was authentic. He was a likable, open and honest manager. He was trusted.

Bjørk's desire was to, "lift the company to a new plateau." He seemed convinced that the organization was ready for something more — something that could energize and empower. What they were contemplating was much broader in scope than minor improvements or short term returns. He desired a major developmental program to revitalize the organization. One that could lead to shifts in attitudes and beliefs and create a basis for continual self-renewal.

Bjørk's desire to "lift the company to a new plateau" triggered the idea that a visionary approach might be most appropriate. Intuition urged me to begin by encouraging Bjørk to create a mental image of what the new plateau might look like. I sensed that if we were to begin with discussions of the goals and content of a new round of management development seminars, or campaigns designed to increase productivity, quality, or cost-effectiveness, then the new plateau would remain elusive. Focusing on any one of these, we could have expected results. My hunch was that in focusing on the new plateau, all of these would be effected.

THE PREMISES

During this first meeting, I began to see that Bjørk and I had similar philosophies about employees' needs, their relationship to the organization, and the kind of orientation necessary to foster self renewal in an organization. We both believed that elaborate mechanisms for strategic planning may give a false feeling of control over the future.

In retrospect, I can say that these shared premises were particularly supportive of the visionary approach and acted as the foundation of the KF revitalization effort:

- KF employees are responsible human beings. They are willing to take responsibility for dealing with all problems related to carrying out their tasks and contributing to KF as a whole. The desire and the potential for each employee to assume more responsibility exists and is waiting to surface. This surfacing is dependent, to a large degree, upon enhancing the development of: positive self-esteem, a proactive attitude, delegation, self-empowerment, and new skills.

- Through their jobs, employees expect to satisfy much of their need for identity, meaning, belonging and contributing to something greater than themselves. Employees have a desire to make a difference.

- Employees are not just a means to the company's ends, they are also ends in themselves. They have a desire to grow and to make use of their innate creative potential. Therefore, the company has an obligation to create the conditions that will allow them to maximize this potential.

- Short-term orientation does not lead to competitive advantage and continual self-renewal. These are dependent on long term perspectives.

While discussing the company's unique competencies, critical challenges and opportunities, I asked Bjørk to describe work situations which excited, angered, disappointed, or pleased him. I was searching for clues to what he cared for most — as a manager and as an individual. These stories revealed that Bjørk was sincerely committed to decentralization and delegation. He also felt strongly about the synergetic potential inherent in the   cooperative effort between the business units of KF.

THE PARADOX

To Bjørk, expressing the benefits of decentralization and of greater integration of the four business units seemed contradictory. If one were achieved, it would probably be at the expense of the other. Decentralization and working together as a whole seemed to represent a contradiction. I suggested that perhaps we were talking about a paradox. Paradox involves seemingly mutually exclusive and contradictory elements being present and operating at the same time. Capturing the essence of a situation or challenge in a two-word paradox can be a fruitful launching point for generating new insights.

I struggled to find two Norwegian words that would capture the essence of the paradox Bjørk was describing. The two words that came to mind were "desentralisert fellesskap." I have yet to find an equally poignant English translation of this two-word paradox. The closest include: decentralized unity, decentralized community, and decentralized connectedness.

The Garden Metaphor

Bjørk had difficulty verbalizing the company in terms of "desentralisert fellesskap." Identifying an analogy is one way to capture a paradox. An analogy is explaining something by comparing it to something else. Nature provides a rich source of analogies. I encouraged Bjørk and Tafjord to search the world of nature for an analogy of this paradox. Letting imaginations roam, we shared the images we were seeing: trees... plants...fields...forests.

An image of a garden appeared in Tafjord's mind and Bjørk instantly recognized the analogy to the paradox. Each flower in a garden is unique. Flowers growing near one another in the garden are collectively unique. The common soil, the bedrock and the underground water system influence each flower and plant in the garden and simultaneously they influence the whole of the garden.

I started making sketches on napkins and bits of paper and soon we were all drawing flowers, green plants, soil, water systems, and insects. These elements of the garden seemed to have their counterparts in the structure and dynamics of the Karmøy plant. We saw the Reduction Plant as one flower, the Rolling Mill another, the Extrusion Plant a third and so on. Each had unique characteristics, structure and form. Each was deeply rooted in and drawing nourishment from the common soil.

As we continued to compare the company to a garden, we began speaking of its dynamics and the conditions for growth as if it were the company. The garden metaphor surprised us with its richness and relevance. The plants had become the individual business units, the insects—the customers, the bedrock—the values, the leaves—the various departments, and the water system—the leadership function.

Noteworthy is how the metaphor helped Bjørk find new meaning in the paradox. Bjørk had described himself as "non-visual and non-imaginative," but suddenly he was able to enthusiastically and vividly communicate his mental images of the company's past and present. Visualizing KF as a garden put us in contact with the very fundamental human and organizational needs of:

- being "apart" and being "a part of";
- being independent and dependent;
- being responsible for oneself and for the whole; and
- of the whole being greater than the sum of its individual parts.

On the plane back to Oslo I was exhausted, yet excited. This encounter had been the most unusual of the initial consultant/client meetings. In three hours we proceeded from introductions to the emergence of a metaphor symbolizing one of the company's central paradoxes. I was overcome by a strong feeling of conviction. Intuitively I knew that the garden metaphor was the vehicle which could help Bjørk describe the new plateau he so wished the company to reach. I felt that proceeding with the visionary approach would help Bjørk clarify a sense of direction and purpose for both himself and the company.

IMAGING:
A FRAMEWORK
FOR VISIONING

The three of us had two more conversations during November and December, 1986. In addition, Bjørk and I had several meetings alone. The garden metaphor was a constant source of inspiration as it helped us to diagnose and visualize complex organizational interrelationships and thereby think more systemically about the organization and its dynamics.

I posed questions designed to access information about the organization's history and current situation. Responses to questions elicited key words, ideas, and issues. These served as springboards for identifying themes pertinent to the visioning process at KF.

Visions are about imaging the future and bringing into

being new possibilities. Imagery is the mental processes of creating sights, sounds, smells, tastes and sensations in the absence of any actual external stimuli.

Imagery is a means of improving communication between the conscious and unconscious levels of the mind as it provides simultaneous access to both levels. It enables people to make contact with the deepest levels of their body, psyche and soul. Our images give us the power to span time. An image held in the mind can affect every cell in the body. Images and physical reality influence each other. Images are a vehicle for profound intuitive insights.

Imagery is less susceptible to personal censorship and can be more revealing than verbal expression. Imagery allows us to express ideas and feelings which are not usually easily accessible. Imagery is an especially useful tool when dealing with tasks which are complex, uncertain and novel, such as visioning. Our images often become more vivid with practice.

Guided imagery is the process of leading someone on an imagery journey. A facilitator suggests a theme and the imager creates a corresponding image.

KF In The Future

Being in a relaxed state of mind improves one's ability to

image. Therefore I taught Bjørk some relaxation exercises. In his relaxed state, I guided him mentally from present to future. Using a theme as a springboard, I would depict a specific scene five years into the future to serve as the starting point for the imagery experience. I would ask Bjørk to report what he was seeing. Five years was used because Bjørk believed it to be far enough into the future to allow for significant changes, yet close enough to motivate. I would then pose a question and encourage the reporting of the ongoing imagery experience. In imaging KF five years into the future, examples of the questions Bjørk was asked to explore were:

- What is meaningful about your work?
- What is meaningful about your contribution to this organization?
- What contributions is KF making to society?
- What difference does KF's efforts make?
- What is KF especially good at?
- How is KF distinctive and unique?
- What added value does KF's customers receive?
- Why are KF's customers demanding its products and services?

- What makes KF different from others in the same industry?

- How is KF helping other Hydro Aluminum plants to become more successful?

These were some of the questions which served as a starting point. As he responded, I continued to pose follow-up questions. It was my role to stimulate the flow of images in a way which seemed most beneficial to Bjørk and the theme he was visioning. As facilitator, I was challenged to pose questions which would free Bjørk's imagination so that creative, relevant and meaningful insights could surface. In navigating such uncharted waters, asking the right questions was of paramount importance. Listening to, and trusting my intuition, served as a guide.

THE LEADER AND VISIONING

When Bjørk addressed questions without being in a relaxed state, he offered less visionary responses. The responses were more likely to be known solutions or projections based on existing facts. After several meetings, I observed that his ability to image increased dramatically. With increased imagery practice, Bjørk was able to image without the use of a formal relaxation exercise.

Bjørk was sensitive to the aspirations and fears of the employees. He was also pragmatic, in tune with business realities, and well focused on the needs of customers and stakeholders. Beginning with that first meeting in October, Bjørk entered a period of intense introspection. During his personal search he experienced uncomfortable periods of confusion and frustration. Bjørk permitted himself to spend time reflecting on what it was he wanted to create as managing director of KF, and in his life. This process was somewhat alien and overwhelming to Bjørk. Alien in that it was new, overwhelming in that it was taking him to a place unknown.

Bjørk's inward journey provided insight, inspiration and courage. These, fueled by the identification and reaffirmation of values, brought the energy needed to create new meaning.

Where were we heading? Would the management group, the union leaders, and the employees be able to relate to Europe's largest aluminum company as a garden? Would the garden metaphor provide insights for others or would they find it too esoteric and alienating?

Those first rough sketches of the 1992 KF garden as Bjørk imaged it, conveyed how company strategy, structure and culture are interdependent. To us, the sketches expressed much more than most lengthy documents which highlight data on market share, return on investment, or other quantitative projections.

Having experienced the empowering effect of visioning,

Bjørk and Tafjord sensed its potential for bringing the organization to a new plateau. They were eager to first involve the management and union leaders, and then all of KF's employees. It was important to do this before Bjørk's own vision was so clear that other perspectives could not be incorporated.

In 1986, the task of creating a vision for an organization was claimed as the sole responsibility of the CEO or the top management team. To my knowledge, large scale employee involvement in a visioning process had never before been attempted.

Adopting a visionary approach with employee involvement was novel. There were no examples to follow. Mistakes would be made along the way. To me, it meant entering into a different kind of client/consultant relationship. It was the difference between focusing on problems and cures, compared to focusing on the organization's potential. I was to be co-navigator helping them to discover what they wanted to create.

I have the very deep conviction that allowing people to express what they want to create is basic and essential to developing individual and organizational potential. It is also essential for achieving and sustaining a competitive advantage. Bjørk and Tafjord shared this conviction. So the decision to invite members of the Working Committees to participate in developing the content of a vision for KF at the already scheduled biennial BU Conference in February, did not feel risky; it felt right.

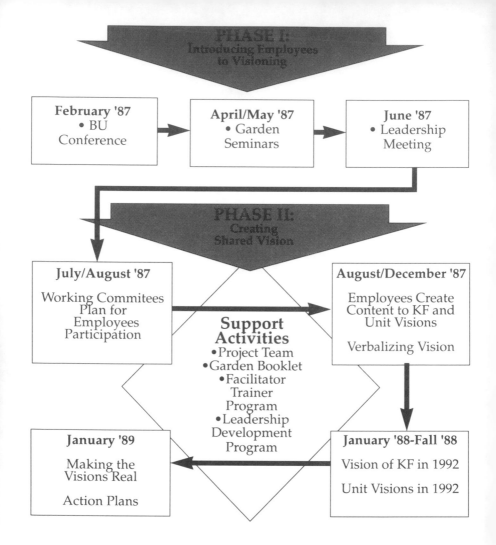

PHASE I:
Introducing Employees
to Visioning

| **February '87** • BU Conference | **April/May '87** • Garden Seminars | **June '87** • Leadership Meeting |

PHASE II:
Creating
Shared Vision

July/August '87

Working Commitees Plan for Employees Participation

August/December '87

Employees Create Content to KF and Unit Visions

Verbalizing Vision

Support Activities
• Project Team
• Garden Booklet
• Facilitator Trainer Program
• Leadership Development Program

January '89

Making the Visions Real

Action Plans

January '88-Fall '88

Vision of KF in 1992

Unit Visions in 1992

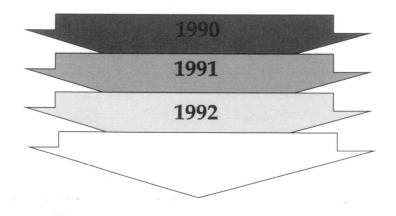

1990

1991

1992

THE VISIONING PROCESS

I t is only in retrospect that the process of employee participation in visioning at KF can be illustrated. We were not following a master plan. Rather, we were being drawn by the power of a shared vision taking form.

Beginning with the BU Conference, many things began happening at KF in relation to visioning. We were not following a prescribed course of action. To make it easier to follow the "process," I have assigned the labels Phase I and Phase II. These phases and the chart illustrating the "process" could only be identified after the fact, in retrospect, the result of the very human need "to process."

Introducing
Employees to
Visioning

I n January 1987, the garden-metaphor existed only as a mental image. To enable others to relate to the metaphor; to use it as a framework and vehicle for visioning, an artist's conception of the garden as Bjørk imaged it in 1992 was needed.

Disappointed with the sketches submitted by artists from two different design studios, Tafjord contacted a local art teacher from Rudolf Steiner School. It was fascinating to observe Bjørk explaining to the artist the character as well as the business realities of an aluminum company in garden language. Drawings were also made of 1987 and 1980 KF gardens to illustrate the relationship between Bjørk's vision of the company in 1992, the company today, and what the company was like six years ago.

From the artist's work it was evident that she understood and captured the intention and essence of the metaphor. The paintings were completed in time for the conference.

K.F. 1980

Siggen Falkeid

KF in 1980

K.F. 1987

KF in 1987

K.F 1992

Liggen Falkried

KF in 1992

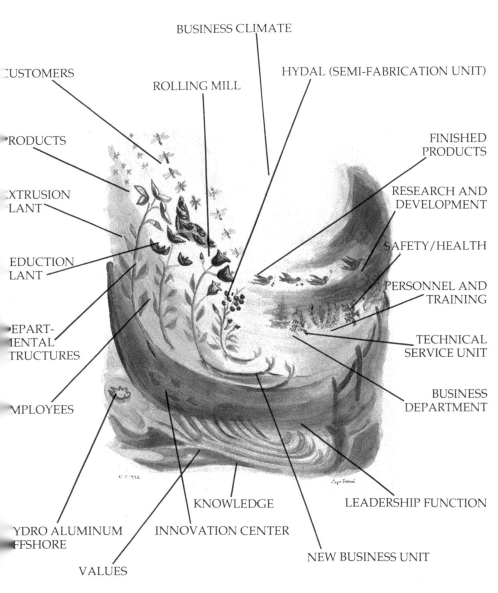

BUSINESS CLIMATE

CUSTOMERS

ROLLING MILL

HYDAL (SEMI-FABRICATION UNIT)

PRODUCTS

FINISHED
PRODUCTS

EXTRUSION
PLANT

RESEARCH AND
DEVELOPMENT

EDUCTION
LANT

SAFETY/HEALTH

PERSONNEL AND
TRAINING

DEPART-
MENTAL
TRUCTURES

TECHNICAL
SERVICE UNIT

MPLOYEES

BUSINESS
DEPARTMENT

KNOWLEDGE

LEADERSHIP FUNCTION

HYDRO ALUMINUM
OFFSHORE

INNOVATION CENTER

VALUES

NEW BUSINESS UNIT

What the KF Garden symbolizes

THE FEBRUARY 1987 BU CONFERENCE

My part in planning the conference was to design a program that would involve employees in the visioning process. I met with the conference planning committee, Bjørk, Tafjord and the staff of the Training Department in working out the final details.

We hoped that by the end of the closing session, each participant would know that the conference launched an effort intended to lift the company to a new plateau.

The two day conference was held at a hotel a few hours drive from KF. The 130 managers and union representatives arrived on the evening before and only an informal supper was planned.

Opening the conference

The chairman of KF's Advisory Committee, Bjørn Nederaas, opened the conference. He mentioned that while previous BU Conferences had focused on KF's problems, this one would focus on its potentials. He expressed his hope that all participants would keep an open mind while exploring entirely new ways of working together. What he was saying had additional meaning when looked at from the perspective of his other post. Nederaas was also vice-chairman of the Ålnor Chemical Workers Union — the largest union at KF with 1200 members.

An introduction to vision

As the next speaker I gave a presentation which touched on:

- proactive versus reactive ways of relating to the future;

- what a vision is and the reason for creating one;

- how visioning differs from reactive ways of relating to the future;

- thinking skills employed when creating a vision;

- the power of mental images; and

- the frustration that can arise when we create an image of something we want but do not know what steps to take to make it "real."

I led the participants through some simple mental imagery exercises, giving them an opportunity to image something from the past, present and future. I selected one of the organization's key values, caring, and led a guided imagery exercise which allowed the participants to image how, in 1992 they personally were embodying this value — from the moment they went through the gates of the plant until they left in the evening. They shared their 1992 images of caring; caring for their co-workers, customers, and physical facilities. I shared my belief that it's not enough to have a framed list of values hanging on the wall. Having mental images of how we manifest our values is what propels us to act.

Message from the managing director

Tormod Bjørk began his presentation by showing three slides of the Karmøy plant — first as a small dot on the globe, then as a somewhat larger dot in Europe and finally as an even larger dot in Norway. He shared reflections about the impact of the company in these three contexts.

He spoke of the need for the company to lift itself to a higher plateau and how this depended on every employee's ideas and commitment.

In Bjørk's words, "We have developed ourselves as an organization but there is the potential for much more. Now we will reach a new plateau. But if we are to do this together, we must think in new and different ways. If we continue to do what we've always done, we'll continue to get what we've always gotten."

The remainder of the presentation centered on slides of the artist's interpretation of the KF-garden metaphor in 1980, 1987 and 1992. He explained how the garden symbolized the unique strategic and cultural strengths of the company. He described what each symbol in the garden represented. Comparing slides of the 1987 and 1980 garden pictures, he described the changes which had occurred during that seven year period, and praised the employees for past and present accomplishments. Comparing the 1987 and 1992 garden pictures, he highlighted the differences. Participants could now emotionally and intellectually identify the gap between the company's present and the potential which Bjørk envisioned for 1992.

My fear that some of the 130 participants would laugh or communicate verbally or non-verbally that comparing their workplace to a garden was absurd, kept me awake the night before the conference. This did not happen. Most looked surprised when slides of the garden metaphor first appeared on the screen. It was Bjørk's sincerity and authenticity that commanded respect and attention. Bjørk was speaking from his heart. He shared the uncertainty he had felt when he first became managing director in the spring of 1986. He also shared his conviction that he had never considered himself to be especially imaginative or visionary, but that his work with the garden metaphor and imaging had helped him to create mental images of a possible and desirable future for the company. Bjørk's message was important because so many people assume that leaders are born visionary and that this is a skill that cannot be developed.

The energy was building, attention was focused. More than words were being communicated. When he talked about the company's opportunities using the dynamics of a garden, he helped the participants recognize important systemic relationships. He communicated in language that was understandable and engaging. Bjørk expressed how bedrock values such as caring, honesty, and openness influence all facets of KF. The dynamics between values (the bedrock), the leadership function (the water system), the structure of the various units (the arrangement and shape of the leaves), market orientation (the scent), the products (flowers) and their quality (form and color), seemed understood.

Each participant could see their unit among the rest of the organization in each of the garden pictures. Bjørk's garden opened up an experience of meaning — a kind of "aha" which comes from realizing at a gut level that one is part of a larger social whole. Not only do individual values, attitudes and actions affect one's own workplace, department and unit, they also affect the whole organization.

Follow-up presentation

My follow-up presentation incorporated the themes of: looking for possibilities in new ideas, the importance of listening and deferring judgement, guidelines for divergent thinking, and some guidelines for visioning.

Through examples, drawings, and humor I tried to create an atmosphere which would encourage participants to experiment and enjoy themselves while imaging the Karmøy plant in 1992. The task of the group discussions was not to create a finished vision. Creating the content of the Karmøy vision would be carried out over an extended period of time and would involve all the employees.

Group work

The participants were told that they would be working in groups the remainder of the day. The next morning each group would share their 1992 visions of KF. They were told to imagine that the year is 1992 and asked to:

- focus on what really matters to them;
- focus on what they want to create, not how to make it happen;
- focus on imagining what is happening; and
- avoid focusing on today's problems and what isn't working.

The participants were asked to imagine what it would feel like to work at KF in 1992: how they, their unit, and the plant as a whole would interact with other units, customers, the local community, and other Hydro-Aluminum plants.

Group discussions

The participants were divided into groups of 15-20 for a short orientation. A member of the Training Department distributed the "Guide to Gardening" booklet. The booklet contained the program for the conference, tips and guidelines for gardening (visioning), and a glossary of the garden symbols. Questions similar to the ones I asked Bjørk were "translated" into garden language.

The groups were told that crayons, felt, flip chart paper, overheads, colored pens, tape, scissors and other supplies were available in each room. It was up to each group whether they made use of this material. The larger groups were then divided into smaller groups of 5-6 members.

After 2 hours of discussions (with a lunch break in the middle), each small group sent two of its members to visit two other groups. Thus, every group was visited by two participants from other groups. This visit to find out what others were talking about lasted about 20 minutes. The "visit each other" intervention was a way of bringing new perspectives and energy into the discussions.

Another one hour meeting in which each small group further developed their ideas about the 1992 company followed the visit intervention. The last two hours were spent in the original large groups of 15-20 people. This time was spent sharing ideas and reaching a consensus about which ideas to present to the rest of the employees the following morning.

Although we did not actively facilitate the group meetings, the staff of the Training Department and I were available to answer questions.

Group presentations

The last session was devoted to sharing the groups' 1992 visions of KF. Presenting the results of their discussion, they were asked to imagine that the year was 1992. They were to speak in the present tense, as if what they envisioned already existed, "The year is 1992 and we are....".

The Karmøy garden came alive. The words fantastic, powerful, and energizing all come to mind. I have worked with the creative process in business for many years. Even so, the creativity demonstrated during these presentations surpassed any experience I have had either as a facilitator or participant. The atmosphere was electric.

The participants expressed their visions of KF in songs, poems, limericks, sketches, collages, models, and drawings so numerous that they could easily have covered the walls of the hotel meeting room. The content of these artistic expressions were clear value declarations. They left no doubt that those present did indeed care deeply about their organization.

These first vision formulations included new and innovative concepts about how the company would sustain excellence. They also encompassed new ideas for information flow, and how KF could interact with its physical, social and business environments.

In closing the conference Bjørk expressed his reactions and hopes: "This has been fantastic. You have shown creativity and displayed abilities which have moved me. This shows that we feel safe with one another and have a strong platform to stand on. Now we must go further. The ideas and symbols you have come up with these past days have made my picture of KF in 1992 richer. But we who have experienced this BU Conference are only a small part of the employees. We must now go back and tell about this conference and explore ways we can involve everybody in creating the future picture of the company we work in."

Conference Evaluation

The Karmøy Advisory Board met shortly after the BU Conference to evaluate the conference and come to a consensus on how the company could best follow up. As impressions were shared, it became clear just how important the experience of visioning had been for them. The conference had not afforded them the same opportunity Bjørk had had for deep and extended reflection, nor for more than a slight taste of imagery. Nevertheless, it was obvious that their first experience with visioning had left them with a desire to act.

I believe that the desire to act was a result of being tuned in to values. Work life takes on new meaning when we are aware of our values — what we care about most. Through the visioning process we gain a deeper awareness of our values. Tuning in to these values we are able to create more meaningful images of the future. When visions and values are in accord, there awakens within us a compelling desire to act. The desire to bring the world in harmony with our visions and values.

Several admitted how skeptical they had been before the conference and how they and other group members had experienced some frustrations during the group work. Now they were beginning to realize that visioning was:

- a proactive approach to addressing the future;

- a way of developing an overarching framework for KF and their unit; and

- an approach which would provide strategic and cultural direction.

They were amazed by the depth of creativity which had emerged. They were surprised by the high level of participation and by the impact the garden metaphor had in stimulating their imaginations.

They were interested in allowing all employees to have a similar visioning experience, an initial training in visioning, before proceeding to allow them to participate in creating KF and unit visions. Several people mentioned how difficult it was to communicate what had actually happened during the conference. The videos taken hadn't captured the spirit of what really transpired.

The Advisory Board decided to give the remaining 1570 employees the opportunity to participate in a one-day conference of similar design. At first I had reservations. One day seemed to me significantly less time than the day and a half of the BU Conference. I doubted that the same involvement and creativity could be achieved in a shorter time frame. I feared that the risk-taking, experimental, and open-minded climate so essential to creativity gradually built up during the BU Conference, would be much more difficult to establish during the course of one short day. An additional concern was the logistics of arranging a series of one-day seminars for 1570 people (3 of the 4 production units work shifts).

Before the meeting ended, my reservations seemed insignificant. I was witnessing the energy of people participating; the energy of visioning. I knew that despite my reservations, the one-day seminars (Garden Seminars) would invoke a similar spirit and release of creativity. Management and union leadership's commitment to the implementation of a novel revitalization approach was indeed genuine.

Inviting employees to participate in visioning is an expression of caring and respect, of appreciation and of believing in the employees' willingness to take responsibility. By inviting people to participate in creating a vision of their work place in the future, Bjørk demonstrated that he felt that every employee was equally important, no matter what their job. It was a demonstration in words and action of respect. Respect, equality and caring inspire trust. All three of these inspire creativity and nurture human potential.

The April-May 1987 Garden Seminars

Preparations

Tafjord mobilized a group of employees to help organize the seminars. The group became known as the Garden Committee. In resolving the question of logistics, it was decided that the seminars would be held at a hotel in Haugesund, a 20 minute drive from KF. The Garden Committee decided that each Garden Seminar should represent a cross section of KF. To best solve logistical concerns, 13 seminars were needed. There were only about six weeks between the first March planning meeting and the first Garden Seminar in April.

Tormod Bjørk wrote to all the employees, inviting them to participate in a Garden Seminar. Although most employees had attended large meetings, employee involvement was usually very limited and meetings tended to be dominated by a few. Most employees had no expectations that these seminars would be different. The overall positive responses to the invitations were lightly peppered with skepticism.

The members of the Working Committees and the union leaders took an active role in encouraging the employees to participate. The involvement and commitment of union leaders stands out as one of most critical factors influencing the success of the early phases of the visioning process.

Union leaders participated in every meeting I had with the management team. I was impressed by their straightforwardness, insight, and the degree to which they showed that they cared about the company and were willing to act. I was also impressed with the courage they demonstrated in stepping out of traditional union roles to work so closely with management. Two union leaders were especially supportive of the visioning process. They were Øyvind Røkenes and Bjørn Nederaas, the chairman and vice-chairman of the Ålnor Chemical Workers Union.

Participation was voluntary. Of the 1570 employees invited, only 300 did not attend. Among their stated reasons were time conflicts, sick leave, and being out of town.

Learning from the BU Conference, much needed to be done before the first Garden seminar. The "Guide for Gardening" needed to be revised and presentations needed to be shortened.

When I arrived at the hotel the night before the first Garden Seminar, Tafjord was supervising the hotel personnel and members of the Garden Committee. There was careful attention to detail along with the anticipatory excitement. Chairs were being arranged and rooms readied with art supplies and garden pictures. Again, I had a restless night's sleep. Some of my initial reservations returned. Could we succeed in creating an environment that would allow creativity to flow? Would we be able to smoothly handle the logistics of moving the 120 participants throughout the day through this maze of a hotel?

A difference between the BU Conference and the Garden Seminars was the established Garden Committee. Not only were the members of the Garden Committee effective organizers, they were also inspirational. As we stood waiting for the first Garden Seminar participants to arrive it was the presence of the Garden Committee that calmed me.

The first Garden Seminar

The objectives and design of the Garden Seminars were basically the same as that of the BU Conference. Following the opening song which was composed and sung by the Garden Committee, I gave my vision talk, Bjørk delivered his message and I concluded with follow-up remarks.

Group work

The members of the Garden Committee served as facilitators and reviewed the guidelines for visioning, answered questions about the garden metaphor, and made suggestions for getting started.

Once the group work began, contact with the groups was limited. It wouldn't be until the presentation stage that we would be able to gauge success. Although impatience caused me to take sneak looks into various group rooms, Bjørk, the Garden Committee, and I, spent most of the day not knowing how things were going.

Group presentations

During my periods of doubt and reservation I had maintained hope, confidence and faith that the Garden Seminars would be successful. Despite this, I was not mentally prepared for the intensely moving experience of watching the evening's presentations. Again, visions of KF in 1992 were expressed in speeches, songs, poems, limericks, sketches, collages, models and drawings. Again, the visions were clear value declarations. They included new concepts for customer relationships, logistics, production and information flows.

Bjørk had encouraged those managers and union representatives who had attended the BU Conference to attend the dinner and to stay for the presentations. Many of them confided to me that they were quite unaware of the extent to which the employees care and have ideas — constructive, new and innovative ideas. Many were especially astounded by observing the creativity of employees they had previously thought were only negative, without opinions or constructive ideas.

All Garden Seminars

After about an hour, most groups experienced a period of frustration. It was a struggle to stay focused on the future (1992) instead of talking about what was wrong with the present situation. This period of frustration was followed by a period of more intense activity during which ideas began to flow. The garden-metaphor served as an aid to opening up the imagination and insights of all but a few groups.

It's interesting to note that as the employees returned to KF with stories of songs, poems, sketches, some of the employees who had yet to attend became apprehensive. Some didn't want to attend because the described activities were ones that made them uncomfortable. The union leaders worked to assure and reassure them that they would not have to do anything they didn't want to do. Each group would design the format and contents of their presentations.

Creativity was expressed in both the content and the means of communicating. Altogether 40 songs and hundreds of drawings about KF in 1992 were composed during the course of the 13 Garden Seminars. All of this creativity was generated in the course of a few hours by employees with no training in creative thinking skills. The diverse groups included both Ph.D.'s and maintenance staff, engineers and line workers, mail room clerks and staff management. It was a moving and humbling experience to witness this demonstration of employees' true commitment to a better KF.

Included in the visions were a number of images of new benefits such as company vacation cottages on the Mediterranean and better company parking lots. A few managers were alarmed, interpreting these as demands. My attitude was that if you invite any group of employees to share how they see their workplace five years into the future, then material wishes will be expressed.

One of the goals of the Garden Seminars was to provide a positive experience in sharing ideas and not having them discredited. Therefore it was important that managers keep an open mind while listening to the employees' presentations, and that they not draw a premature conclusion that most of these ideas were designed to meet the employees's "ego" needs. If managers began to identify ideas as demands, their emotional reaction (in most cases negative) would block their willingness to discover the potential of each idea.

Divergent thinking involves mentally opening up for new and unusual possibilities. It involves the discovery of new relationships existing between previously unconnected elements. Convergent thinking involves analyzing possibilities and developing selection criteria. It involves improving and refining promising alternatives, and ultimately it involves making effective decisions and judgements.

In order to present their visions at the Garden Seminar, the employees had to use some convergent thinking skills in deciding the content of their presentations. The convergent thinking was limited to a show of hands as to what should and should not be included.

Visions, like creative solutions, are dependent on both divergent and convergent thinking. Although these were not intentionally included in the seminar design, I was aware that employees would need to learn converging techniques which would include the development of selection criteria. Convergent thinking training would be part of the next phase.

The visions of KF in 1992 expressed the employees' convictions about how best to relate to customers, suppliers, the local communities, schools, retired employees and the environment. Also included were descriptions of technical excellence, performance commitment, leadership, flatter hierar-

chy, information flow and union and management cooperation. The visions expressed how each department and unit
were drawing nourishment from and providing nourishment to the whole of KF. All of these 1992 themes were
expressed in the present tense.

THE JUNE 1987 LEADERSHIP MEETING

A few weeks after the last of the Garden Seminars, Bjørk
invited KF leaders and union representatives to a two-and-a-
half day off-site meeting. The challenge to be addressed was
follow-through. Now that the employees had experienced
and been introduced to visioning, how could each unit implement the next phase of the process? How could each unit
develop the content of a shared vision of KF and their unit?

Preparation

I was asked by Bjørk to develop a program for the leadership meeting including the theme of follow-through, as well
as a number of other issues. We hoped that after the meeting
the participants would leave with:

- a better understanding of the potential of visioning
  as an approach to organizational revitalization;

- an improved ability to share this understanding
  both inside and outside the organization;

- clarity about their own role in the next phase of
  the project and a desire to commit to it;

- an overview of challenges likely to arise and strategies for dealing with these;

- an awareness of the forces influencing the revitalization effort and of the importance of monitoring them; and

- an understanding of how to create an environment supportive of the revitalization effort.

I had hoped to give the participants an experience in developing personal visions, and to spend some time discussing how to deal with stress that often accompanies change. Regrettably, there was not enough time to include these topics.

The Meeting

During the meeting I introduced techniques to aid in divergent and convergent thinking. I helped participants identify factors in the present situation (such as beliefs, attitudes, behaviors, systems) which could support or block the outcome of the next phase of the project. Divergent and convergent thinking was used in developing and deciding upon criteria for organizing employee involvement and gaining acceptance for proposed plans.

Need for action

Bjørk had told everyone attending the Garden Seminars that the process of involving hundreds of employees in visioning could take many months. Major changes should not be expected before the process was completed. Nevertheless, within a short time many employees were wondering how long it would take before they could act upon some of the more concrete aspects of their visions. They were impatient. Their impatience was positive as it indicated there was a strong impetus to start creating the future today.

The leaders decided to act at once on some of the more concrete aspects of their visions. This was an expression of respect; it signaled to the employees that their creativity would be taken seriously. The implementation of some ideas affecting their own workplace need not wait until the KF-vision and unit visions were fully formulated. Some ideas could and should be implemented immediately.

CREATING SHARED VISION

C reating shared vision, Phase II, refers to the time period from July 1987 to the fall of 1988. During this period employees throughout the company were involved in working together to create the content of a vision for KF, for their own unit, and in some cases, for their own department. It was during Phase II that plans to communicate and act on the visions were developed.

This phase of the revitalization effort began with each Working Committee planning how to involve their employees in creating the content of the visions.

This is an example of how one business unit organized its work:

> *The Working Committee appointed an ad-hoc committee consisting of both union and management*

representatives. Their first task was to sort the materials from the Garden Seminars, including handouts, videos, drawings, overheads, models, songs and other materials produced by the employees of that unit. This material was sorted by department, according to those ideas which were so short-term and concrete in nature that they could be dealt with immediately.

The Working Committee asked each department within the unit to appoint a contact person. The ad-hoc committee was to ensure that the contact person received copies of all Garden Seminar material that was relevant to their department. The ad-hoc committee was also to provide any additional help the departments might need to continue visioning discussions.

Each department was more or less free to decide if they wanted to carry out their visioning discussions during or after the work day, and if they preferred an on, or off-site meeting place.

Of the nine Working Committees, one did not participate in Phase II. A business unit with 130 employees was experiencing serious economic problems. As a result, their management team was reluctant to participate. Since the concept of visioning was still so new to KF, I respected the decision to postpone participation in the process. Many of the employees in this unit were disappointed they would not be continuing the visioning process.

The thinking processes central to visioning can also be applied to issues confronting an organization in crisis. Visioning and creative problem solving can be powerful tools in creating win-win solutions. Today, I regret not having had the opportunity at that time to help this unit experience the potential of imagery in creating and exploring possibilities. Some months later I did have the opportunity to help Bjørk and two others envision a solution to a crisis confronting this unit.

From August to December 1987, departments and work groups met together to generate content to KF's visions. To support their work were The Project Team, The Facilitator Training Program, and The Leadership Development Program.

The Project Team

While the overall responsibility for the revitalization effort remained with Bjørk and the responsibility for implementation remained with Working Committees and line managers, a Project Team was established. The objectives of the team were:

- to keep informed as to how visioning was progressing throughout the company and to update Bjørk;

- to ensure that when the KF vision was finally

formulated, there would be effective ways of communicating it throughout the organization; and

- to initiate actions which would help all units move in the direction of the 1992 visions.

Bjørk appointed a union leader, a manager of one of the larger units, two employees from the Training Department and Tafjord as members of the Project Team. Tafjord was appointed chairperson. As external consultant, I reported directly to Bjørk, but served as an advisor to the team.

The Facilitator Training Program

The need for a group of trained internal facilitators to help with Phase II had become increasingly apparent. Twelve employees were invited to participate in a two day Facilitator Training Program. Mostly these were the same persons who had been members of the Garden Committee. They were from various units and job ranks and all possessed some natural networking and facilitation skills. Facilitator functions included:

- providing advice and inspiration to groups that were having problems with the visioning process;

- serving as facilitator in meetings where there was a need for external help;

- teaching work groups idea generation (divergent) and idea development and evaluation (convergent) techniques; and

- giving feedback to the Project Team about what seemed to be working or not working.

The purpose of the Facilitator Training Program was to help facilitators gain a deeper understanding of group processes and visioning. The participants received some basic training in facilitative skills and creative problem solving techniques.

In subsequent one and two day programs, they were given the opportunity to discuss the experiences they were having in their role as facilitators.

THE FALL 1987 LEADERSHIP DEVELOPMENT PROGRAM

To insure that a large number of managers and union leaders would be able to identify with the revitalization effort and acquire attitudes and skills supportive of it, an extensive Leadership Development Program was initiated during the fall of 1987.

The Leadership Development Program was a two part program designed for 170 line managers and union representatives. Part one of the program started in the fall. Ivar Njerve from the staff of the Training Department was organizer and trainer. He was assisted by the facilitators who had taken part in the facilitator training program.

Participants spent time clarifying values and discussing a new role for leadership. The values given highest priority were: good health, a meaningful work place, and a balance between work and family life.

Following the first seminar, each participant chose a project which challenged them to explore ways they could contribute to bringing KF closer to their 1992 visions. Part two included a module for sharing experiences from the visioning process in their own work groups and a module for learning convergence skills. From the many ideas generated it would be necessary to reach consensus on what would be included in the verbalized vision as well as which ideas would be acted upon. To aid in idea selection, the participants were introduced to convergent thinking. Unless managers learned the skills to converge, ideas targeted for action would have to be selected by others, thus eroding the shared visioning process.

Partly as a tool for convergence, and partly as a way to illustrate shared vision from an integrative perspective, I developed a simple model (see figure, next page).

At the center is the core: the organization's purpose, assumptions of human nature, values and uniqueness. The core of an organization is like the character of an individual. Increased awareness of our core helps us discover who we are, what we stand for, and what contribution we want to make in the world.

The core is the foundation of the organization's distinctiveness in relation to both culture and business. When the focus of our vision is the whole organization, it is important to ask ourselves questions which help us image aspects of the core — as we would like to see it manifested.

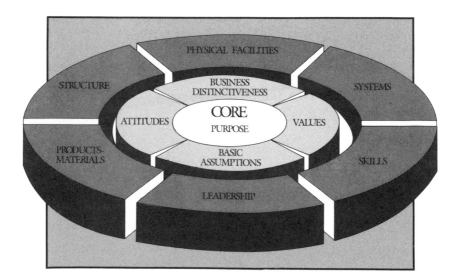

•Environment •Market •Society

For a vision to be a powerful force "pulling" an organization to its future, the mental images must reflect how the core manifests itself in the future. Visions are images of how we see our purposes unfolding. (See figure, next page).

THE GARDEN BOOKLET

In addition to the support work of The Project Team, The Facilitator Training Program and The Leadership Development Program, a booklet was produced to help address the purposes and nature of visioning at KF. The booklet outlined:

- why KF started a revitalization effort called "KF in the Future";

- what a vision is;

- reasons for creating a shared KF vision;

- the meaning of the garden metaphor; and

- ideas for creating the content of a vision.

Also included in the booklet was an illustrated version of the phases of the visioning process; and the 1982, 1987, and 1992 pictures of KF as a garden with descriptions of the state of the company at these times.

The booklet came off the press in mid-fall. This was later than intended and too late to benefit those groups who were near the end of their discussions. Less ambitious but more

Vision of Organization

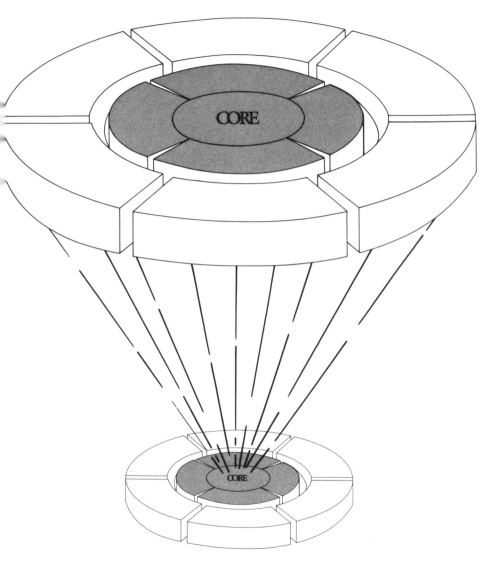

Organization Today

frequent communications, such as a newsletter, might have contributed more to supporting employee efforts.

OWNERSHIP OF THE EFFORT

The active role of the Advisory Board, the Working Committees, the managers, the union leaders, the Training Department, the facilitators and the Project Team along with Bjørk's continuous expression of commitment to the revitalization effort, all served to reinforce company ownership. Because of their involvement, the revitalization effort was "owned" by the company and not the external consultant.

As external consultant, the challenge was to maintain a balance in the dichotomies of being: empathetic/confrontive, sensitive/prodding, intuitive/systematic, spontaneous/structured, idealistic/pragmatic.

My clients and I were close. We shared excitement, joy and laughter while creating a living model of shared vision. The challenge for me was to maintain a relationship with my clients that was close enough to facilitate sharing yet distant enough to remain objectively effective.

I visualized desired outcomes of meetings, interventions, and the steps that were needed to be taken to achieve these results. Seldom was I completely satisfied with myself. After a meeting or intervention, alternatives that could possibly have been more effective came to me. I fretted and worried.

Although I was guided by my intuitions, there were times when I couldn't communicate them effectively enough and therefore abandoned them when faced with resistance. I was determined to maintain a facilitative style and therefore shied away from directive behaviors. Perhaps some obstacles could have been avoided or lessened, had I been more persistent.

At times I was frustrated and irritated, mostly with myself but now and then with my clients. From time to time I felt at odds with my clients. The Project Team felt strongly that each unit management team should work alone synthesizing their unit's visions. On the contrary, I believed that the process would be aided by additional interventions.

Several unit managers had been promoted to corporate level positions and transferred from KF. I feared that the new managers who came during Phase II would have trouble identifying with the process. I was convinced that each manager would benefit from having a deeper experience with visioning, one more similar to Bjørk's.

I also felt that unit managers could benefit from help integrating corporate guidelines for strategy development with the visioning approach at KF. A haunting fear was that business strategy would be developed independent of visioning, that strategy would be considered one thing, and visioning another.

I was concerned that unless leaders were taught to antici-pate and understand the range of emotions that this process unleashes in everyone, that fear would lead them to resort to behaviors that undermine the process. Visioning unleashes conflicting forces in people. Feelings of hope and inspiration are often followed by fear and anxiety as the realization that we have to change behaviors becomes increasingly evident. In order for learning to occur, we have to recognize how our own emotions are contributing to creating our current reality.

I remained at odds with the Project Team and therefore had to accept less involvement during what I considered a critically important phase. It wasn't easy. It was painful to hear stories of how some managers felt frustrated and con-fused. Hearing of employees' disappointments because things weren't happening fast enough or because management be-havior was inconsistent with what was being said, concerned me. I cared deeply.

Although one part of me yearned for a phone call from a Working Committee or a unit management team asking for help, another part of me was reassured that they'd find their own solutions. Out of the frustration, they'd learn. My rescu-ing in the short run might have diminished their ownership in the long run.

VERBALIZING VISION

F ollowing the plans of their respective Working Committees, the employees had been working in groups since August of 1987 to create the content of their visions. During this time I frequently asked myself, "What does the written manifestation of a vision look like?" Having experienced the powerful effect of the 1992 garden metaphor, my undisclosed desire was that everyone in the company would at some time be able to express the KF vision and a vision for their own unit using the garden metaphor as a "living" symbol.

I knew that this was unrealistic. Although some groups were using the garden metaphor to facilitate their visioning, most did not. My impression was that the Garden Seminars did not give the employees enough exposure to the garden metaphor to allow them to comfortably use it in their visioning meetings. Too much time had passed since employees attended the Garden Seminars to when they again began visioning in their own work groups.

There were groups of employees who were very keen on using the garden-metaphor to help them create content to their visions, but would stop doing so if one or two of their group members were negative. Negative group members suggested the process was too impractical or not concrete enough.

The potential of the metaphor, so strongly evident during the BU Conference and Garden Seminars, was never fully realized. It had been an extraordinary vehicle for opening up imaginations and insights. It had provided a common language and a means to understand the interrelationships, both internal and external, to the organization. It had served an important purpose.

The consensus was that the visions of KF and each unit should be formulated in words and not just symbols. We all hoped that the written KF and unit visions would capture the essence of what the employees had imaged.

CRITERIA FOR WRITTEN VISIONS

Most of the written visions I read in management literature seemed like cliches to me. I am aware, however, that vision statements often do appear to the outsider as cliches. The cliche appearance does not make the vision less meaningful if the process used to develop it has been meaningful and if the visions are alive in the mind of the visionary. It is the act of creating the vision, the sense of purpose elicited, the direction it gives and the desire to act which empowers. Powerful visions:

- describe a preferred and meaningful future state; evoke images in the minds of others;

- give people a better understanding of how their purpose could be manifested;

- can motivate even in hard economic times and in times of conflict;

- are perceived as achievable;

- are genuine and come from the heart; and

- are lofty, challenging, and compelling.

Keeping the above in mind is a challenge for anyone trying to formulate concise written vision statements. Written visions should be short and easy to read. They should not include statistics or statements of methods for achieving the vision.

Visions should be expressed in the present tense. Using future tense phrases such as "we will..., we shall..., and we must become..." describes intention and therefore the statement has no logical connection with today. Expressing images of a desired future state in the present tense forces us to look at the vision in relation to today. Present tense forces the question, "How?" It causes creative tension to emerge and brings the vision into motion.

I suggested that they avoid the competitive phrases of being best, first, or number one. Statements such as these can move an organization forward only so long as they are not achieved. Once an organization becomes best, first or number one it is left without a guiding vision. The once powerful vision is transformed into a defensive vision of protecting their number one position. The competition becomes the focus of their energy, and possibilities not related to the competition stand in danger of going unnoticed.

Cause for Concern

I received word that instead of using guidelines for visioning, some groups of employees were generating content to KF visions by brainstorming.   An effective vision is not the product of a brainstorming session. The vast quantities of ideas which were the product of brainstorming sessions were most often short-term goals.

I created a form for work groups to sort ideas according to theme, and which should be included in the written KF vision, in unit vision or departmental visions. For those groups of employees who had used brainstorming, going through their material and sorting out their statements according to theme was difficult and frustrating. They also discovered that in many cases questions dealing with the "core" of their department, unit and KF vision had been partly overlooked and additional meetings were needed to address these important aspects.

THE VISION REPORTS

Groups submitted their completed vision statements to their Working Committees. The Working Committees then assembled them in report form to be submitted to the Project Team.

The reports of the Working Committees' visions for KF in 1992 began reaching the Project Team in mid-December 1987. Reading them was an experience almost as inspiring and moving as that of witnessing the presentations during the BU Conference and Garden Seminars. Each report included new and innovative concepts about how the units and KF could be sustaining excellence in a wide variety of ways. The character of the statements generated was both visionary and action oriented.

The reports were additional evidence of a high level of employee creativity. Bjørk, Tafjord, the Project Team, the management team, and union leaders spent many hours reading through these reports, gaining insights into how hundreds of employees envisioned the company in 1992.

The Project Team appointed a group of five, myself included, to go through all the reports and extract those visions that related to the whole of KF. We then drafted a written vision for KF in 1992 which Bjørk could edit. His draft would be sent to each unit management team and each Working Committee for discussion and modifications.

THE MARCH 1988 MEETING OF TOP-MANAGEMENT AND UNION LEADERS

Bjørk invited the KF leaders to yet another two-and-a-half day off-site meeting. A year had gone by since the February 1987 BU Conference. During this time several of the managers had been transferred to other parts of the corporation. This meant that each time I met with this 21 person group I encountered new faces.

One of my challenges in planning this meeting (as well as the previous ones) was finding ways of establishing psychological safety, rapport, support, and trust. This was particularly important for new members. Risk-taking behavior and not being afraid to make mistakes are integral to the success of a revitalization effort. Group cohesion supports such behaviors, and with frequent changes in leadership, cohesion is difficult to maintain.

Bjørk presented a revised draft of the "Vision of KF in 1992." The managers agreed that more work needed to be done to develop a clearer vision of the 1992 KF core.

A guided imagery exercise helped the participants image what KF as an integrated aluminum company could offer its customers in the way of added value, both tangible and intangible. Not having applied imagery to this particular issue before, I was amazed when the participants revealed how easy and exciting it had been for them to break fixed mind-sets and image new and innovative concepts for business development, some of which could be incorporated into the vision.

Among the other issues discussed were how to integrate the strategic development activities which were going on at corporate headquarters with unit visioning activities; and an update on ideas and action steps which had already been initiated or implemented as a consequence of the visioning process.

VISION OF KF IN 1992

During the months that followed, Bjørk made another draft of the KF-vision and sent it to the unit management teams and union leaders for comments. It was then printed and distributed to all employees. Each unit management team was responsible for ensuring that the visions for their own unit would be formulated and communicated before summer (1988). This deadline proved unrealistic and three of the unit visions were not printed and communicated until several months later.

I had one-day meetings with Bjørk and a few of the unit managers. Everyone expressed how frustrating and tedious it had been to formulate in clear sentences the essence of their own, and their employees images, of their unit in 1992.

The visions were communicated to the employees in different ways — brochures, newsletters, meetings. The "KF in 1992" garden picture was printed in the yearly almanac. Large-scale versions of the "KF in 1992" garden picture were printed and made available to all employees. About 1300 employees now have this picture in their homes.

MAKING
THE VISION REAL

G iven the kind of organization we envision, what are the appropriate structures, systems, and skills for that organization? How do they differ from our current structures, systems, and skills? What steps are necessary to move us from where we are today to that which we envision? These were some of the questions that managers and union leaders needed to address.

"Making the vision real" is in itself a somewhat contradictory expression. Once you have created a powerful mental image of a desired future state, in one way it is already real. Our images of the future exist in the present in our minds. If these images are aligned with our values, stir within us a sense of purpose, and make sense in the market place, then they are so real that they will engage both our emotions and our intellect. They are so real that they will create within us an irresistible urge to act.

In the spring of 1989, the KF Safety Inspector gave his explanation as to why the accident rate had been reduced by more than half. He said, "A lot more people here are just taking responsibility for their own health." The employees at KF participated in a visioning process in which they envisioned good health as being manifested in 1992. Behaviors and attitudes which contribute to reducing the gap between the vision of good health (including an accident-free work environment) and the current situation are a natural consequence.

Planning in a vision organization becomes a learning process in which perspective continually shifts between our vision and immediate actions. In shared visioning, both managers and employees manage with the image of the desired future state in mind. Ideas surface to anyone for whom the vision is "real".

If a shared visioning process has been successful, in the sense that employees have created, shared and agreed upon which mental images of the desired future state they are willing to commit to, then what follows is that people: a) start living the vision today through their behaviors and attitudes; b) start sharing ideas for taking action; and c) discuss alternative action steps which can move them in the direction of their vision.

There is no one right way to create the future today. There are only more and less successful actions, all of which provide opportunities for learning. As one action step nears completion, new ideas for action are being created in people's minds, assuming they are keeping the vision alive. Changes may seem minute, but the overall effect is one of an organization in constant motion. Employees do not have to be told of the necessity of becoming change-oriented, they are continually in change — continually creating change.

At KF, considerable time passed between:

- the employees' initial participation in creating the visions; to

- the visions finally appearing in printed brochures; to

- a "formal" discussion of action plans in the units; to

- the first "formal" action steps being taken.

For some units this time period extended over a year and a half. The accomplishments of the employees during this period were remarkable and attracted considerable media attention.

The paradox is that while initiatives were being taken all over the organization, or in Bjørk's words, "The company is bubbling with activity," the perception among employees seemed to be that nothing much was happening in connection with the revitalization effort called "KF in the Future".

Because thinking patterns are so ingrained in established planning modes, most employees had difficulty perceiving their own visions as real and existing in the present. The tendency was to presume that most of the time we are doing what we are supposed to do — our everyday job, and now and then we have discussions related to visioning.

Despite the fact that there were many changes taking place all over the organization, these were not formally linked to the visioning process. These changes were in accordance with the vision. But since there were no formal action plans for these day-to-day activities, there seemed to be no logical explanations for the improvements that were taking place.

During Phase II, Ivar Njerve and the Training Department collected news from all the different units. They tried to find out what was happening, what ideas were being implemented, and what employee's reactions were to what they had experienced thus far. Their findings were reported in the *KF Garden News* newsletter which was produced monthly.

In 1989, each unit went about the task of making KF's and their own vision more formally real by developing steps for action. What seems clear is that employee participation in developing action steps was almost as extensive as it was in creating the content of the visions. Instead of trying to use my own words to describe how they went about this process, I have reprinted a couple of *KF Garden News* articles.

HYDAL: THIS IS HOW WE WORKED

Here at Hydal we started our work with a meeting of our management team, where an overall plan was developed which we presented and got acceptance for in our unit Working Committee. After this the real work with the action plan began.

It was natural for us to divide the work between the production and sales departments and make a plan consisting of two parts. Although we have functioned as two independent groups, our action plans nevertheless have many common elements.

We sat together some afternoons and evenings in order to meet the deadline, but also in order to avoid being disturbed by the telephone. We worked a lot in small groups. Those who naturally work together daily were placed in the same group. The various small groups gave priorities which they presented to the other groups. We altogether gave a final priority of action steps. We experienced that it was difficult to take into consideration everybody's desires and viewpoints.

We have all had the opportunity of giving priority to what we feel is important and when we ought to start up the various action steps. Therefore we all want to do whatever we can to achieve the goals we have set.

Through this work with developing action plans, we experienced that we have gained more understanding of visioning and why we should work with "KF in the Future".

After we finished with our action plan, we presented it to the Working Committee. For us, the Working Committee is a driving force which at regular intervals has the action plan on its agenda.

Important to us:

Working together to develop an action plan has made the vision more alive and understandable for us. The action plan has allocated work tasks and the responsibility for implementation of Hydal's vision to many persons and thereby created commitment and satisfaction among many more.

PERSONNEL AND TRAINING DEPARTMENT

Our work with developing action plans has been a continual process since the Management Meeting in Solfonn (March, 1988). Before we started working, we went through the material from the Garden Seminars and the vision report from the Working Committee. Inger S. Tafjord presented the KF and the KF Service visions.

With this as a basis, developed the content of an action plan. The issues we finally agreed to take action on are a combination of old and new ideas, all of which are seen in light of the visions.

We have worked in groups by department and across departmental boundaries. All of the employees have been involved in this process.

The activities which are included in our action plans are divided into two categories. The short-range action steps are concrete and described in detail, while the long-term action steps are more open and general. For each activity we have the name of someone who is responsible, and we have set deadlines for when the actions are to be finished. Our action plan has been printed in 100 copies. Mostly, they were distributed to all the employees in Personnel and Training and to the management of KF.

Our biggest challenge now is to make sure that the action plans are translated into actions. We are therefore concerned about (ensuring) a systematic follow-up of the plan.

These articles show that the employees in these departments were very much involved in creating action steps. Making the visions real depended on employees committing to, and deciding on, action steps, not on management dictating what steps would be taken. For a shared vision to be real, to come alive, the employees must be involved and committed.

REFLECTIONS

Visioning and Change

Has employee participation in visioning at KF made a difference? Is KF more profitable? Was employee participation worth the effort? These are among the questions people are asking today.

Nothing that happened at KF happened in a vacuum. The shared visioning process was nurtured by the foundation of trust that had been established between management and union leaders in the early 1980s. Market conditions took a turn for the better in 1988, resulting in higher aluminum prices and an increase in sales. The production capacity of the Karmøy smelter was increased in 1987. Corporate restructuring also had an impact.

The plant was doing well in 1986 when Bjørk took over. Bjørk could have taken an easier road and focused on maintaining the level of success KF had already reached. Instead, he sought to revitalize the company; to bring it to a new plateau. The employees were invited to envision that "plateau" and to take action which could bring them closer to their desired future.

During the two years I worked with KF, our discussions were not focused on ways to increase profits. The focus was toward developing an organization with more life, more meaning and more direction. An organization which could nourish the creative potential of its employees. Visions focused on how employees see themselves interacting with each other and their physical resources; how they are serving their customers and society in unique ways.

VISION BECOMING ACTION

Record breaking has become a part of everyday KF life. Higher productivity, reduced emissions, lower energy consumption, and higher electricity yield are a few examples of the where records are broken almost every month.

Operating profit in 1986 was 1.59 million kroner, by 1989 it had soared to 1.089 billion kroner. The rise in aluminum prices cannot explain the entire increase. Productivity has increased 33% from 1986 to 1989.

KF received the Norwegian Environmental Award in 1988

for its efforts in reducing pollution. After receiving this award KF didn't stop. Today their emissions are less than 50% of the required government standards.

In 1986 KF had an accident rate of 14 per million working hours. At KF the accident rate in 1989 was 7. Each internal KF news publication reports how an increasing number of departments have been accident free for an extended period of time. Absenteeism at KF in 1989 was 4.8%.

A KF manager reasons that the positive decline in the accident rate and absenteeism is because of: "Participation and self-responsibility. We're not preoccupied with fixed goals, we recognize that it's all about a continual process of improving ourselves".

A worker in the Reduction Plant shared: "We now show that we care for each other. To point out a mistake isn't regarded as something negative, but more as a help to prevent accidents in the department. Everyone is their own safety inspector".

Groups of employees in different parts of KF are actively working to improve their diet, lose weight, quit smoking and to improve their overall physical well being. They are taking responsibility for their own health and safety.

KF implemented a suggestion system in the early 80's.

Ideas for improvements have risen from 131 in 1983 to 1218 in 1989. The benefits from the suggestions exceeds millions of kroner.

Employees are committed to learning new skills. There was a marked increase in employee interest in continued education following the Garden Seminars. Employees want to do their jobs better. They requested and have begun taking courses in foreign languages, chemistry, physics, math, communication, creative problem solving, sales and negotiation skills. They ask for courses which can help them better understand how customer needs, quality, economy, health, environment, safety and performance are interrelated. They want to understand factors that affect their own and their units' results.

A certification program for production workers now gives production workers increased knowledge and skills through additional schooling and on-the-job training. It has uplifted their status. Being a worker on the production line is considered high-quality work.

Extensive leadership development programs have contributed to increased awareness of the role of leadership in the KF of tomorrow. In the fall of 1988 Ivar Njerve initiated a two-year program for managers at all levels. It consisted of 12 two-day modules including modules on economics, group process and communication, planning, line manager's responsibility for personnel, team building, meeting skills, customer relations, health and lifestyle, creative problem solving, and personal visioning.

Njerve also developed an intensive two year leadership development program for a smaller group of potential top-level managers. This program has since been adopted by corporate headquarters and a program of similar design is now offered to all of their Norwegian plants. Njerve is coordinating this effort. Developing creative thinking and personal visioning is integrated into the curriculum of this program. The program is a part of a large scale Competency Development Program at Hydro Aluminum.

A portion of the KF vision reads: "Everyone has access to the information they need to perform their tasks, make decisions, and understand they influence every part of the organization."

More information and training is giving workers access to the information they need to take on additional responsibility. In addition, work has been started to install an integrated data base system and an electronic mail system. Work is also being done to develop a KF network in which parts of each unit's planning systems will be integrated.

Information stands are located at 10 different places around the grounds of KF. These are interactive videos allowing anyone to get up-to-date information on what's happening at KF.

During the Garden Seminars in 1987 some employees described KF in 1992 as a company in which employees were sharing in KF's profits. The personnel director and union leaders worked together to develop a bonus system, not just based on profits, but also decreased pollution, increased safety and other criteria relevant to a particular business unit. The system went into effect during the summer 1988. This has not resulted in workers feeling pressured to produce more at faster rates. Rather, it has stimulated interest in their being aware of the many factors that influence results.

The trend at KF has been toward a flatter hierarchy. Having fewer organizational layers is possible because employees have easier access to the information they need and increased skills to understand it as a result of training. Today there are more group leaders and less foremen. Employees are more directly involved with improving productivity in their areas. They have been given responsibility because they have demonstrated that they have the competence needed to be more closely involved.

VISIONING IS PERSONALLY REWARDING

Although technology, capital investments, new administrative systems and restructuring are what receive credit for changes and results, the fact remains that there are real people behind each of these. People whose ideas have been developed, shared and acted upon. People who in some way have envisioned a new reality.

The following articles appeared in KF Garden News during the spring and summer of 1988. They highlight what the work has meant to the employees of that department:

WHAT HAS THE WORK GIVEN US?

The work was time consuming, created uncertainty, provoked conflicts and occasionally irritation. But, at the same time, we have been involved, felt the challenges and the excitement of paving new roads, discovering new resources and through conflicts came to an understanding and a sense of fellowship. Through this we have come together as a team that's playing in the major league.

We have an action plan which we are proud of. Most important of all is that this process has created clarity, given us goals and a new perspective to our work, and thereby a greater (feeling of) security than before. We know where we are, and not least, we know where we want to be.

It is the vision which has given us this direction. It is, in a way, under our skins. Perhaps unconsciously, but nevertheless, not further away than that it continually pops up and provides new direction to our actions.

This "pathfinder" has also become a source of inspiration and courage, and has already shown its usefulness in practice. The visions are not utopian dreams, but important values which we can incorporate in our daily work.

From the employees in the KF postal service:

During our work with the vision reports we discovered how important it is that we discuss thoroughly how we want our department to be in the future. By working in this way, we get ideas about how we best can organize our work in ways which are best for our "customers" and those who work in the department.

Our way of running meetings is a lot like the way we used when working with our visions, and as we gradually have become used to it, we notice how much creativity we all (as people) actually have.

The Impact of Visioning

Being told to change feels threatening. As a consequence of employee participation at KF, people there don't need to be told to be more change oriented. They are living with change. It's becoming a natural state for them. They are taking responsibility for change. Their attention is focused on what they want to create and not on becoming change oriented. Today's problems are no longer the sole focus. Employee participation in visioning leads to more employees: taking initiative, demonstrating proactive attitudes, using their creative potential, and assuming responsibility for themselves, their units and KF.

Behind the statistics are people whose ideas have been developed, shared and acted upon. People who found new ways of working together, new and faster ways of delivering their products to their customers. People who are saying: "Why are we doing it this way? Maybe there is another way."

KF is today a plant that is visited by many. People both within and outside the aluminum industry are interested in learning the key to KF's successes. KF employees who offer visitors an explanation very often say, "It's because we've started to think differently. We've started to make continuous learning a way of life."

Employee participation in visioning has taught people a

new way of thinking and a new way of relating to the future. They are taking responsibility today for shaping their future. The many changes that have and are today taking place are building the foundation of an organization more capable of self-renewal. Employee participation in visioning has enhanced KF's capacity to create and take action. KF is becoming a learning organization.

People Make
the Difference

What was it about KF that made the visioning process successful during the early phases? Of all the many factors, it was the people that made the difference.

The managing director's personal development positively affected the early phases of the visionary process. During our initial meeting, Bjørk revealed that he felt uncertain about how to best lift the company to a new plateau. Admitting this was, I felt, very positive. He seemed open for alternatives and not bound by preconceived notions and traditional solutions. He acknowledged that in his previous managerial positions he had focused mostly on problem solving, dealing with crisis situations, and keeping the system running.

Bjørk recognized that the insight and skills needed to champion an organizational revitalization process were not a part of his previous work experience. Nor were they taught at the engineering university he attended. He was aware that his formal education and the management seminars he had attended had emphasized rational, logical and analytical techniques and skill development.

I am convinced that the change effort's early successes can be attributed to Bjørk's evolution as a more visionary leader. I heard both managers and union leaders saying in amazement, "Bjørk has really changed!"

As a leader, Bjørk developed a deep intuitive feel for the complexity of the organization. Imagery is a vehicle for profound intuitive insights. Intuition is a useful tool when uncertainty is great, precedent is lacking, facts are few, and predictability is low. As a source of vision, intuition is valued as a means to gain a sense of the future and its possibilities. Bjørk was open and accepting of his intuitive insights.

I do not believe that having a visionary leader is a prerequisite to starting a visioning process. Rather, I believe an organization needs people in top management who are willing to learn to develop their innate capacity to become visionary. An organization needs managers who are sincerely interested in listening to other people express their visions.

The manager of KF's Training Department, Inger Tafjord, was instrumental in starting and sustaining the early phases of the revitalization effort. Tafjord can be described as a holistic thinker, a natural organizer, a challenger of the established system, and a prolific innovator. All of these qualities were critical to beginning a change effort of the magnitude of the one at KF.

The involvement of the union leaders was crucial to the success of the shared visioning process. Several union leaders admitted that they had been criticized by union members both inside and outside KF. Critical to the success of the revitalization effort was the fact that the union leaders:

- didn't back down in the face of resistance;
- stepped out of the "we" and "them" mentality and into one of "we are all in this together";
- participated in the planning and organizing of all the phases of this revitalization effort; and
- were active in encouraging union members to participate in visioning.

All the factors that were critical to the early successes have one thing in common: committed people. The success of the visionary approach to revitalization depended on the people involved. It depended on the leadership, it depended on the unions. Shared visions cannot succeed without the involvement of the people who make up an organization.

CHALLENGES FACING VISIONING

My experiences at KF have made me aware of the challenges facing visioning. I am not just thinking of challenges such as resistance to change that all organizational development efforts have to deal with, but additional challenges perhaps more specific to visioning.

Most people do not have a self-image of being visionary. A lifetime with no encouragement to use imagery, of underestimating the value of imagination, of not reflecting on values and purposes, all reinforce the myth that ordinary people are not able to create visions.

The visioning process can be psychologically stressful. The pull toward the future, at times, has to compete with past behavioral habits. This may result in inconsistent behaviors and emotional swings. One day there's excitement about the future and the next day there's pessimism.

At KF it's obvious that it has been very difficult for some to unhook themselves from past behavioral patterns and attitudes that need to be left behind in order for KF's visions to become reality.

Portions of the KF visions demand the use of skills and behaviors that are not among the many which are represented at KF today. It takes time to learn new skills and behaviors. Most important in working through this psychologically stressful time is to maintain the belief that new skills and behaviors can be learned.

Most people are willing to practice a sport in order to improve their game. However, many do not show the same persistence needed to develop intuitive and visionary thinking skills. Because vision has appeal doesn't mean we can be good at it right away. Many managers at KF gave up before visionary thinking became a natural supplement to their analytical problem solving skills.

A revitalization effort using visioning is not comparable to a "project". KF named the interventions carried out in 1987-89 "KF in the Future". It was useful to have a label for it. The downside of this was that many believed that since it had a starting point and a Project Team, it, like any other project, had to have a termination. When a campaign or project ends, it's natural to ask, "What's next?"

Managers who talk about visioning at KF as a campaign or project limit the potential of vision. What managers believe about visioning may well become a self-fulfilling prophecy. If they believe that employees' ability to create mental images of a desired future for KF is "over with", that visioning is a one-time activity, "what we did when Bjørk was around", their expectations about visioning as an approach to organizational renewal will be lower. Their own lower motivation will lead to reduced effort to keep visioning alive and to use it in connection with other day-to-day challenges.

Visioning is not somewhere "out there". It does not reside in the air, or as a statement in a brochure, or in one artist's interpretation of the KF-Garden. Visions are alive and real in the minds of those visioning.

Visionary thinking skills, when used in conjunction with convergent thinking skills evoke creative solutions. Bringing in outside productivity experts to tell the organization how they should reduce costs tends to short-circuit the creative and innovative potential of shared visions. Bringing in outside experts that "have all the answers" might be interpreted by employees as a lack of confidence in their ability to create new and cost-effective solutions.

The success of shared visioning at KF is dependent upon

rising to the challenge of being true to the founding premises. Interventions inconsistent with the premises of the revitalization effort will cause people to become cynical, resulting in reactive or aggressive behaviors. Both managers and union leaders have told me that there are people at KF today who are disappointed. They have reacted strongly to the lack of follow-up and to inconsistent management behaviors. Some feel that they have been manipulated.

An important key to continual enrichment of shared visions is the development of personal visions. It has been my experience that personal visions include the dimensions of family, organization, community and world. Personal visions express the influence individuals image they will have in these dimensions. As shared vision evolves, "my" vision merges with and emerges as "our" vision.

Visioning is a never ending process. It involves continual motion and evolution. Shared visions depend on commitment. Commitment to shared vision comes in recognizing our personal visions in the shared visions. A challenge of a shared visioning process is to encourage the development of personal vision.

CHALLENGES FACING MANAGEMENT

A constant challenge to the visionary approach to revitalization is its novelty. KF managers and union leaders did not find it easy to explain the nature of the revitalization effort to corporate headquarters. They could not promise immediate results. They were met by considerable skepticism and little overt support. The garden metaphor was subject to some ridicule. This lack of support and encouragement had several negative consequences. Some managers chose to downplay the importance of visioning when they were conversing with corporate headquarters, others chose not to talk about it at all. Still others "sat on the fence", waiting to see whether it had potential for success. Unnecessary time and energy were spent wondering what the executives at corporate headquarters might be thinking, how they might react, and what should be shared or not shared.

KF's moving in the direction of its visions is dependent on management's commitment. If the energy and creativity evident among the employees at KF shall continue to flourish and be channeled in the direction of the visions they helped to create, then management at KF today must be acutely aware of their role as leaders in a vision-driven organization. Leadership behaviors are just as integral to the success of the revitalization effort as employee participation was to the success in creating the content of the shared visions.

Each manager and union leader has to be honest about whether they identify with the underlying objectives of the revitalization effort, the premises and values on which it was based, and the values described in the visions. In the implementation phase, when the task is to design new structures, systems, learn new skills and acquire new behaviors, management's role is critical.

Some managers fear that their career advancement opportunities may be influenced negatively if they do not give top priority to solutions that yield short-term measurable results. These managers may directly or indirectly back away from taking steps which are congruent with the priorities in their visions. A lack of congruence between what a leader says and does will affect the trust level. The trust level will decline rapidly if employees perceive incongruence.

CHALLENGE OF CONTINUITY

Nothing happens in isolation. In January 1989, Bjørk was asked by corporate headquarters to spend a year troubleshooting at another aluminum plant. Immediately after he returned he was promoted to Marketing Director at corporate headquarters. In other words, only a year and three-quarters after Bjørk gained both management and union commitment to this revitalization effort, he was challenged to take on new responsibilities. Inger Tafjord was transferred to corporate headquarters to head the Competency Development Program and left KF shortly after Bjørk.

Several KF employees shared their feelings that Bjørk and

Tafjord's leaving would not be critical to the success of revitalization. They reasoned that the process was decentralized from almost the very beginning. Each Working Committee and management team planned and organized for employee participation within their own unit and had developed action plans. Therefore, whether or not KF and each of its units moves in the direction of their visions is not dependent on any one individual.

Creating the conditions under which this process could be self-sustaining was part of the design. The fact that the process was decentralized distinguishes the KF effort from other companies in which the CEO alone developed a vision, communicated it, and then left.

Although this is true, organizational revitalization requires the sustained attention of a fairly stable group of highly committed leaders. The KF revitalization effort could have been much more effective had it not been confronted with a continual loss of key managers. It could have benefited from a higher degree of group cohesion among top management.

It would be naive to underestimate Bjørk's role in this revitalization effort. Bjørk was typical of most managers in that he was used to focusing on daily operations and statistical analysis. As he developed his visioning skills he became a transformational leader and his ability to articulate what he cared about and to inspire others increased significantly. As a transformational leader he could more easily help groups use vision. He was able to use visioning skills to help groups work through differences and to ensure that new systems and structures were in alignment with the vision.

Facing KF Challenges

To help assure that this pioneer effort does not become just another well-meant but short-lived attempt to involve employees in actively influencing the future, challenges must be met squarely.

KF leaders should look for opportunities to communicate and celebrate small successes. New ways of working, of interacting with customers, with other departments/units, with the local community, in addition to those ideas which improve processes, products and services should be credited to the employees. Internal publications and news releases should attribute successes to people, not to the "organization", or the "system". Internal publications should make it clear how new projects, programs and progress support KF's visions becoming reality. In crediting people with progress, we reinforce their behaviors and provide them with an opportunity to see how they are responsible for influencing their own future.

There should be frequent, honest and open discussions about what is or is not happening today. Without an ongoing awareness of today's reality, visions lose their power. What forces (behaviors, norms, systems, structures, ways of working together, decision-making processes, information flow, and corporate guidelines) are supporting movement in the direction of the vision? Which ones are blocking progress? Which are in conflict? Unless people understand how they are contributing to creating their current reality, they don't see how they can work towards changing that reality. Spending time looking for scapegoats in the "organization", the "system", "policies" or someone higher up is destructive; it prevents learning.

Managers should be evaluated on their commitment to their unit's and KF's vision as it is demonstrated through their daily actions and priorities.

KF should find ways of communicating to new employees the history of KF's visioning approach and the new employee's role in developing the skills, attitudes and competencies which are at the core of the vision. Training should be provided in personal visioning so that the shared vision can continue to grow and to guide the organization.

POTENTIAL OF
SHARED VISION

W hat has my experience with KF taught me about the potential of shared vision? The first words that come to mind when I ask myself about the potential of vision are: purpose, empowerment, focus, creativity, equality and integration.

PURPOSE

Those managers and employees at KF who, through the visioning process, have a clearer understanding of their own, their department's, their unit's, and KF's purposes are able to choose more effectively the steps they need to take to achieve their visions. Their visions become the picture of how they see their purposes unfolding as they move into the future. Their actions contribute to the realization of the vision and the fulfillment of purpose. In connecting with their sense of purpose they give themselves a reason for being and become more conscious of the choices they need to make in order to serve that purpose.

It is a profound, spontaneously growing sense of purpose that orients individuals towards their vision and empowers them to interact effectively with the world around them; it makes vision a reality. Without purpose, vision all too often becomes an impossible dream that may never be realized. The processes of visioning help us get in touch with our sense of purpose.

EMPOWERMENT

Empowerment is a process of enhancing the possibilities for people to gain mastery of their own lives and the decisions that affect their lives. Empowerment involves individuals developing the competencies, abilities, or skills they need to have successful interactions with others. It has to do with the capacity to act in accord with others to fulfill one's potential rather than against others. When we feel empowered we are willing to take responsibility for our situation, recognizing that we are part of a larger social whole. It means taking responsibility for the success of our work place, unit and company. Participation in creating a vision, in developing action plans and taking steps to implement the plans all enhance empowerment.

FOCUS

Creating the conditions by which people can feel empowered without creating the focus provided by a vision can lead to an organization without direction. It may produce movement, but without any direction. It can create movement without alignment.

A shared vision provides focus. It can align the energy in an organization. It can prevent employees from dissipating their strengths in a variety of unrelated directions.

COMMITMENT

Most people sense that tighter controls and tighter supervision are not the answer needed for companies eager to develop an innovative environment. Simultaneously giving greater freedom and expecting greater commitment seems paradoxical. A vision, provided it is effectively communicated, easily understood and "alive" in the minds of the employees can replace close supervision. The need for rules and threats is reduced. When it is our own vision, one we ourselves have created or contributed to creating, the potential for commitment to it is increased.

If our physical, psychic, mental and emotional energy becomes channeled into something which has greater meaning, we commit to it. The supervision comes from within.

CREATIVITY

Creative processes enhance visioning and visioning processes enhance creativity. Creating a powerful mental image of a desired future state which is different from the reality we recognize in the present, stimulates a desire to act.

As soon as a desired future state comes closer to reality, there is a need to create another desired future state. The vision and the present reality are always "in tension". This means we are always creating with the intention of developing further, of serving a higher purpose. This situation promotes ongoing creative thinking. Creative thinking becomes a "habit"!

Additionally, since there is no one way of achieving a vision, our creativity is constantly spurred on. We have to: make and communicate meaningful new connections; be able to see new and unusual possibilities; generate and select among a variety of alternatives.

The ability to be innovative is a primary determinant of business success. Vision and visioning processes have helped a large number of employees at KF develop skills critical for successful innovators.

EQUALITY

Equality has to do with openness, respect, and acceptance. When Bjørk invited the employees to participate in visioning, he was communicating that "we are equal experts on the future."

The garden metaphor provided a common language. Employees could communicate as equals because their individual education, background and position in the company was immaterial. Everyone's uniqueness and individual qualities could be included and contribute to enriching the visioning process.

INTEGRATION

A shared vision has the potential of being an integrating force in organizations. It can be a mechanism for coordinating the efforts of groups with diverging interests. The garden-metaphor and the various processes used in visioning helped Bjørk and some others to intuitively "grasp" the whole, or the "big picture". Their intuitive insights gave them not only an intellectual understanding, but an emotional realization that each individual, each department, each unit, is responsible for themselves and for the whole KF-community. They understood that it is possible to achieve an equilibrium between, and to strengthen the dynamics of interdependence and autonomy. They were able to embrace that paradox.

Conclusion

Has the visioning process at KF led to: purpose, empowerment, focus, creativity, equality and integration?   I have experienced glimpses of each. Walking through KF today and talking with employees, a visitor will also experience glimpses of these being manifested. Enough to recognize that in both subtle and overt ways some of the potential of visioning is now embedded in KF's culture, they are affecting KF's results.

The unique blend of people, history, and organizational culture has led to the way KF has embraced shared visioning. Each individual, organization or group that begins visioning processes must come to terms with their uniqueness. For a vision or shared vision to be compelling, it must reflect the unique blend of values, people, purpose, history, environment and culture. It is not possible to duplicate another's vision or visioning process. Each organization must identify their own paradoxes and their own metaphors.

Shared visioning depends on commitment, which is the product of recognizing and embracing uniqueness. We can learn from others' visioning processes, but we cannot duplicate them.

Now and then I ask myself, what really happened at KF? What was it that really kindled those moments of energy, creativity, meaning, focus and for some, true vision?

The Latin root of the word spirit is spiare meaning "to breathe". The word inspired is also a derivative of spiare. One who is inspired is one in whom the spirit is strong.

Spirit has to do with the feelings each individual has about the meaning of who they are, of what they are doing, and of the contributions they are making. Spirit is what has influenced KF's remarkable achievements. More goes on at KF than meets the five senses; spirit is that more.

The BU Conference and the Garden Seminars are two examples of an intense and visible outpouring of spirit. However, three years after these events, KF is still full of spirit. Even in those parts of the organization where things appear tedious and humdrum, people are full of spirit.

My experience at KF has convinced me that individual and organizational spirit is nurtured and strengthened by being in touch with values, having a clear sense of purpose and a compelling vision towards which actions are directed. Creating shared vision fosters the spirit in the organization. It is spirit that fuels continual renewal and constant improvement.

Managers, consultants, and others who are searching for ways to inspire and to create the conditions under which people are inspired, have to be willing to take the in-depth journey of nurturing and strengthening their own spirit.

ABOUT THE AUTHOR

Marjorie Parker is an organizational consultant, co-founder and senior partner in the Norwegian Center for Leadership Development based in Oslo, Norway.

A native of Rochester, Minnesota, Ms. Parker worked first with international organizations in New York, the Middle East, Germany and Norway before taking a position as project manager with the Norwegian Institute of Urban and Regional Research in 1968. She shifted from research to training and consulting in 1976.

Ms. Parker was awarded a national scholarship from the Norwegian Council for Leadership Development in 1984. In 1989 she received a stipend from the Norwegian Council for Scientific and Industrial Research to document her work with using innovative approaches to leadership development and organizational change.

She has designed and conducted creative strategy workshops for management and project teams in many of Norway's leading corporations. Considered a pioneer for having introduced creative problem solving, lateral thinking and imagery to Norwegian business, Ms. Parker continues to be an enthusiastic promoter of creativity in business. She speaks at international business conferences and has published in the management and business press.

Ms. Parker has a B.A. in political science and a M.Sc. in Creative Studies.

Please send _____ copies of *Creating Shared Vision* at $14.95 per copy as soon as possible.

Orders must be pre-paid in US dollars. Books will be shipped fourth class book rate.

Within US: add $3.00 for the first book; $.50 for each additional book.

Outside US (surface): add $4.00 for the first book; $1.00 for each additional book.

_____ book(s) at $14.95 per book: _____

6.75% sales tax (IL residents only): _____

Shipping & handling: _____

Total enclosed: _____

☐ Check payable to Dialog International Ltd. enclosed.

☐ Charge my: ☐ Visa ☐ MasterCard

Card # _____

Signature: _____ Exp. _____

Name: _____

Organization: _____

Address: _____

City: _____

State: _____

Zip Code: _____

Phone: _____

Mail orders to: Dialog International, Ltd.
1220 N. Fair Oaks Ave.
Oak Park, IL 60302

Fax orders to: (708) 323-4962

ISBN # 0-9630000-0-4

ADDITIONAL READING

LEADERSHIP/ ORGANIZATION / TRANSFORMATION

Adams, J.D. (Ed.) *Transforming Leadership: From Vision to Results.* Alexandria, VA: Miles River Press, 1986.

Bass, B.M. "From Transactional to Transformational Leadership: Learning to share the vision". *Organizational Dynamics,* Vol.18, Nr.3, (Winter 1990), pp. 19-31.

Beckhard, R. and Harris, R. *Organizational Transitions: Managing Complex Change.* Second Edition. Reading, MA: Addison-Wesley Publishing Company, 1987.

Bennis, W. and Nanus, B. Leaders. *The Strategies for Taking Charge.* New York, NY: Harper and Row, 1985.

Block, P. *The Empowered Manager: Positive Political Skills at Work.* San Francisco, CA: Jossey-Bass Publishers, 1987.

Brimm, I.M. "Risky Business: Why Sponsoring Innovation May be Hazardous to Career Health". *Organizational Dynamics,* 1988, 6, (3), 28-41.

Burcke, W.W. *Organization Development: A Normative View.* Reading, MA: Addison-Wesley Publishing Company, 1987.

Conger, J.A. T*he Charismatic Leader. Behind the Mystique of Exceptional Leadership.* San Francisco, CA: Jossey-Bass Publishers, 1989.

Davis, S.M. *Future Perfect.* Reading, MA: Addison-Wesley Publishing Co., Inc., 1987.

Fitzgerald, T.H. "Can Change in Organizational Culture Really Be Managed". *Organizational Dynamics*, Vol.17, Nr.2, Autumn 1988.

Fritz, R. *The Path of Least Resistance*. New York, NY: Fawcett Columbine, 1989.

Hagemann, G. *The Motivation Manual*. Aldershot, Hants, England: Gower Publishing Company, 1992.

Harmon, W. *Global Mind Change. The Promise of the Last Years of the Twentieth Century*. Indianapolis, IN: Knowledge Systems, Inc., 1988.

Hickman, C.R. and Silva, M. *Creating Excellence. Managing Corporate Culture, Strategy and Change in the New Age*. New York, NY: New American Library, 1984.

Hickman, C.R. *Mind of a Manager. Soul of a Leader*. New York, NY: John Wiley & Sons, Inc., 1990.

Kilman, R.H., Covin, T.J. and Assoc. *Corporate Transformation. Revitalizing Organizations for a Competitive World*. San Francisco, CA: Jossey-Bass Publishers, 1988.

Kuhn, R.L. (Ed.) *Handbook for Creative and Innovative Managers*. New York, NY: McGraw Hill Book Company, 1988.

Land, G. and Land, V.A. *Forward to Basics*. Buffalo, NY: D.O.K. Publishers,Inc., 1982.

Leavitt, H.J. *Corporate Pathfinders. Building vision and values into organizations*. Homewood,IL: Dow Jones-Irwin, 1986.

Mastenbroek, W. A "Dynamic Concept of Revitalization". *Organizational Dynamics*. Vol.16, nr.4, (Spring, 1988).

McWinney, W. and Batista, J. "How Remythologizing Can Revitalize Organizations". *Organizational Dynamics*, Vol.17, Nr.2, (Autumn, 1988).

Miller, W.C. *The Creative Edge. Fostering Innovation Where You Work.* Menlo Park, CA: Addison-Wesley Publishing Company, Inc., 1988.

Morgan, G. *Riding the Waves of Change. Developing Managerial Competencies for a Turbulent World.* San Francisco, CA: Jossey-Bass Publishers, 1989.

Morgan, G. *Images of Organization.* Beverly Hills, CA: Sage Publications, 1986.

Pascale, R.T. *Managing on the Edge.* New York, NY: Simon and Schuster, 1990.

Schaef, A.W. and Fassel, D. *The Addictive Organization.* San Francisco, CA: Harper & Row, 1988.

Schein, E.H. *Organizational Culture and Leadership: A Dynamic View.* San Francisco, CA: Jossey-Bass, 1985.

Senge, P.M. *The Fifth Discipline.* New York, NY: Doubleday/Currency, 1990.

Tannenbaum, R., Margulies, N., Massarik, F., and Assoc. *Human Systems Development.* San Francisco, CA: Jossey-Bass Publishers, 1987.

Tichy, N. and Devanna, M.A. *The Transformational Leader.* New York, NY: John Wiley & Sons, Inc., 1986 Vaill, P.B. Managing as a Performing Art. New Ideas for a World of Chaotic Change. San Francisco, CA: Jossey-Bass Publishers, 1989.

van der Erve, M. *The Power of Tomorrow's Management. Using the vision-culture balance in organizations.* Oxford, England: Heinemann Professional Publishing Ltd., 1989.

CREATIVITY / IMAGERY / INTUITION

Agor, W.H. (Ed.) *Intuition in Organizations. Leading and Managing Productively.* Newbury Park, CA: Sage Publications, 1989 .

Amabile, T.M. *The Social Psychology of Creativity.* New York, NY: Springer-Verlag, 1983.

Bastick, T. *Intuition- How We Think and Act.* New York, NY: John Wiley & Sons, 1982.

Bolnick, M. "The Interface between creativity and cognitive dissonance theories". Ph.D. Thesis, University of Michigan,1983

Diebold, E.B. "An Investigation of the Functional Properties of Guided Imagery". Ph.D. Thesis, University of Michigan,1986.

Durio, H.F. "Mental imagery and creativity". *Journal of Creative Behavior,* 9, 233-244, 1987.

Galyean, B.C. *Mind Sight. Learning through imaging.* Long Beach, CA: Center for Integrative Learning, 1983.

Goldberg, P. *The Intuitive Edge. Understanding and Developing Intuition.* Intuition. Los Angeles, CA: Jeremy P. Tarcher, Inc., 1983.

Grønhaug, K. and Kaufmann, G. (Eds.) *Innovation: A Cross-Disciplinary Perspective.* Oslo, Norway: Norwegian University Press, 1988

Howe, M.A. "Using Imagery for Problem Solving in Organizations in Different Stages of their Development". Ph. D. Thesis, University of Michigan, 1985.

Isaksen, S.G. (Ed.) *Frontiers of Creativity Research. Beyond the Basics.* Buffalo, NY: Bearly Limited, 1987.

May. R. *The Courage to Create.* New York, NY: Bantam Books, Inc., 1975.

Miller, E.E. *Software for the Mind.* Berkeley, CA, Celestial Arts, 1987.

Ornstein, R. *The Psychology of Conciousness.* New York, NY: Viking, 1972.

Sheikh, A.A. (Ed.) *Imagery: Current Theory, Research and Application.* New York, NY: John Wiley & Sons, 1983.

Wheatley, W.J.,jr. "Enhancing Strategic Planning Through the Use of Guided Imagery". Ph.D. Thesis, University of Michigan, 1985.